PARENTS & LIFEGUARDS

UNITE TO SAVE LIVES

Lessons Learned for Safer Swimming

By:

John J. Moore

DEDICATION

Water sports and other water related recreational activities are great sources of fun and fitness. This book is dedicated to the safe enjoyment of those activities by every child and everyone charged with the care and safety of those children in and around this nation's swimming pools. All of my stories have happy endings.

Please make sure your stories are happy too.

TABLE OF CONTENTS

1 - <u>INTRODUCTION</u>

My lifeguarding career began over 50 years ago. My parenting career began almost 40 years ago. In the early days of my lifeguarding, I focused on the "saving," part of my job with over 100 "saves." As a parent, I learned more about prevention. My two daughters became lifeguards too. And now as a grandparent, I am "<u>all about the prevention</u>."

Those saves I've made occurred mostly in pools but also in a lake and the Atlantic Ocean. Accordingly, this book will focus on the activities in and around swimming pools, but the principles apply to all bodies of water. And to be clear, when I am referring to "parents," I mean anyone overseeing the safety of a child. That could include friends, grandparents, older siblings, other relatives and baby sitters.

Having observed the behavior of both lifeguards and parents at a variety of aquatic venues over the years, I have concluded that both have a lot to learn from each other. And if they do learn these lessons many tragedies will be prevented in the future.

The following are a series of very short stories about what happens in and around swimming pools. They come directly from my personal experiences and observations. These examples demonstrate many lessons we all can learn about preventing water related tragedies.

For parents, here are 4 very important steps in preventing a swimming accident with your child:

1. Learn to swim
2. Teach your children to swim
3. Watch your children
4. Watch some more

(Numbers 3 and 4 are the most important steps for all parents to remember)

And remember, too, lifeguards are your "backups," _you are the first line of defense for your children._

For lifeguards, here are 4 steps to ensure the safety of those you protect:

1. Stay alert and focused without distractions
2. Anticipate
3. React to any and all concerns – seconds count
4. Know that common sense is all too uncommon

Additionally, remember that accidents have happened in a pool just like yours and that "it" can happen at any time.

Note too, that this is not a book about statistics, but rather, a book about accident prevention through lessons learned.

2 - <u>LIFEGUARDS ARE HUMAN TOO</u>

The sun was shining bright. Not a cloud in the sky and there was a good crowd at our family camp that day. It is a popular camp with many activities for all, including a lake and two swimming pools. One small pool for wading and another larger pool as well.

Several lifeguards were on duty and they would rotate from one guard stand to another about every half hour and take breaks periodically. John was the "Head Lifeguard" with a lot of experience and he knew just how important it was for all the guards to be alert and ready for anything at any time. John was always watching all the swimming areas as well as the guards who were on duty.

There was one guard that John was watching very carefully that day. Derek was a new guard. This was his first day on the job. He had recently completed his lifeguard training and was fully certified to work as a lifeguard at a pool but he was not yet certified to guard at an open waterfront. So, John kept him working at the pools.

At about 11:30 that morning John was sitting on a picnic table about 10 yards away from the larger pool and somewhat between the two pools so he could watch the activity at them both. He was talking to another guard who was off duty when he noticed something unusual about Derek's behavior.

Derek was sitting in an elevated guard stand when John noticed that he stood up and grabbed his whistle in his left hand. Then Derek sat back down again. And then he stood partially up and halfway down. John could tell that something must have caught Derek's attention, but by his hesitation, it was obvious that he was unsure as to what he should do.

3

To John, with his experience, this was a sign that was not all that uncommon for a new lifeguard. Just like a "rookie" in any field, one can have all the very best training possible and pass all the tests with flying colors but make mistakes and fall short in the first true test on the job. No one can truly know how he or she will react in that first real emergency.

John immediately ran over to the pool and asked Derek what was wrong. Before Derek could respond, John saw what it was. Two young teens were submerged below the surface of the water together in the deep end of the pool. Both of them had been swimming and playing happily just moments before. The 12 year old boy had a seizure, causing him to stop swimming and a 13 year old girl attempted to help him. Unfortunately, she was not strong enough to keep him up and they both sank.

John dove right in and pulled both to safety at the side of the pool. She was fine immediately. It took a little longer for the boy to catch his breath but he too was fine. John thanked the girl for trying to help but recommended that, if this should ever happen again, she should call out to the lifeguard for help rather than taking on the risk herself.

After everything settled down, John took Derek aside to make sure that he learned from this experience. The lifeguard training dictates that, **"IF YOU DON'T KNOW – GO!"** That means that it is better to "go" and save someone who does not need saving than to not do it for someone who needs saving. For Derek, the good news was that he recognized a swimmer in distress. The next time, he will not hesitate. He will "GO."

****

Another human condition facing lifeguards besides inexperience is the fact that at times the job gets pretty boring. It is a monotonous activity coupled with the heat and glare of the sun. It is possible to lose concentration. A guard can get fixated on one thing for too long and essentially "zone out" on the big picture while focusing on one area.

****

PARENTS: Your supervision is important even when there are lifeguards at the pool. While lifeguards do save lives, often prevent accidents and enhance safety, they do have limitations.

LIFEGUARDS: Be alert. Get your proper rest. Constantly be moving, both physically and in your scanning. If you find yourself losing concentration, have another guard relieve you so you can take a quick dip in the pool. And always remember – **"IF YOU DON'T KNOW – GO!"**

3 - <u>PAY ATTENTION</u>

Here we are back again at our wonderful family camp with the two pools and a lake on another nice day. It was not a very busy day so our lake was closed as the two pools were able to accommodate the number of swimmers that day.

The beach is really not very big, although the lake is large enough for all kinds of water activities including fishing, water skiing, sail-boating and jet-skiing. We share the lake with other camps as well as area residents. Our sandy beach only goes back about 10 feet from the water where there is a two rail fence with an opening in the fence where bathers enter and exit the beach area. When the lake and beach area is closed, as it was that day, there is a rope strung across that opening with a sign hanging from it stating that the area was "closed."

Head Lifeguard, John, glanced down the hill from the pools toward the lake when he observed a very dangerous situation developing. Sitting on a blanket on the grassy area between the pools and the beach was a young couple. They were sitting approximately 20 yards from the beach. Their young toddler was walking toward the beach. In fact the toddler was about 5 feet from the beach, which meant he was only 15 feet from the lake water that was not protected by any lifeguards since it was closed.

Given their location, relative to the child and the water, that child could have easily worked his way under the rope and into the water before the parents could reach him. John was too far to run down the hill and stop this accident from happening. So, he blew his whistle several times as loud as he could. The noise appeared to stop the child as he turned around and it got the attention of the parents too. John pointed to the toddler in an effort to get the parents to get the child before he could go on the beach.

The father did retrieve the child in time but neither parent had been paying enough attention to recognize the potential danger developing right in front of them.

****

Lifeguard John was walking around the wading pool when he looked down and saw the panicked face of a little girl standing completely submerged as she looked up and reached for a friend's arm standing next to her. He immediately jumped in and lifted the girl out of the water to safety.

Her name was Kathy and she was playing in the wading pool with several other friends. Kathy was very small compared to her friends. The wading pool goes from 2 feet deep to 3 feet deep. She and her friends were having fun playing in the shallow end and in the middle, where there was a fountain, spraying water. As her friends moved deeper and deeper, Kathy tried to stay with them by bobbing off the bottom of the pool to keep her head up above the water. But as she neared the deepest end of the pool, her friends became separated from her and out of her reach, just when she could no longer bob to breath.

As John pulled her out of the water, her mother came running to her and thanked him for helping her daughter. Kathy's mother had been sitting and talking with friends at a picnic table not far from the pool. Her mother, knowing that Kathy could not swim, apparently had not noticed the pool's water depth which was clearly marked. Additionally, she was unaware that, as her friends went into the deeper end, the water would be over her daughter's head.

****

As Lifeguard John was guarding at our local pool, he observed a young girl, maybe 3 or 4 years old playing in the water by the stairway at the shallow end of the pool. As he looked for this girl's parents or someone who might be with her, he saw her mother standing outside of the pool about 5 feet away from the pool's steps talking and laughing with friends. As he watched this little girl in the water, who cannot swim, has no floatation device on and was playing where she could easily slip or be knocked over by others as they come in and out, he was thinking to himself, "what is this mother thinking?"

What happened next, just floored John! He explained to this girl's mother that she needed a floatation device, should not be in the water by herself and cannot play on the steps. This was her mother's exact response: <u>"Oh, whenever I see you guys in your red shirts, I don't see that word "lifeguard," I see the word **"Babysitter"** spelled out across your chest."</u> She was laughing the whole time as she said this, apparently in hopes of impressing her friends.

John was not impressed and calmly explained to her that she would have to go in the water with her daughter or take her daughter out of the pool. The mother was not wearing a bathing suit and obviously had no intention of going swimming, so they left.

****

Whatever happened to "common sense?"

PARENTS: Please watch your children and don't be distracted by activities like reading, playing cards, texting, mowing the lawn, talking on the phone or with others. Know how deep the water is. Know your child's limitations. Remember, lifeguards are your backup. You are the first line of defense for your child. Pay attention.

LIFEGUARDS: Be on guard for the unexpected. Don't expect others to have the same level of interest and concern about water safety issues. You have been trained to think about these things. What may seem to be common sense to you, unfortunately, is not so common to the general public.

4 - <u>ANTICIPATE</u>

Wow! There was a lot going on at the pool that day and it was a perfect day for it. Not only did we have a good crowd with our regular swimmers and some new ones too. We were conducting lifeguard training at the same time, adding about a dozen swimmers plus a couple of instructors.

Lifeguard John was sitting in the elevated guard stand at about the middle of the pool with the deep end to his right and the shallow end to his left. Much of the lifeguard training was going on next to John on his right in the deep end and just outside the pool on the deck.

John was scanning the pool as we lifeguards constantly do, when he noticed 4 year old Christine in the shallow end of the pool. She and her family are regulars at the pool and John knew she could not swim and that she could just barely stand up there. Knowing the family as he did, John would have anticipated seeing her little sister and their mother close by. Normally, her mother was in the water or sitting nearby at the side of the pool. He did not see her mother anywhere. But what he did see was not good.

John saw Christine's little 2 ½ year old sister, Abby, walking on the deck toward the edge of the pool. She had both arms out stretched toward her older sister. Abby normally wore a "puddle jumper" but she had no floatation device on at all. She had a great big smile on her face as she walked right into the pool, jumping on top of her sister.

Anticipating the calamity about to happen, John jumped down from the guard stand before Abby even jumped into the water. The lifeguard instructor standing next to John immediately covered for him by watching the rest of the pool to protect the other swimmers. While not planned, this turned out to be a good learning opportunity for the lifeguards in training who were able to see a near double drowning as it happened and then watch the save as it was being made.

As Abby jumped into the water, her sister tried desperately to help hold her up, but she immediately lost her balance and both of them went under water. John ran around the side of the pool to the shallow end, jumped in and pulled both girls up and out of the water. They were scared but fine otherwise. All of this took place while there were several swimmers and adults within arms' reach but no one even noticed until John jumped in.

Their mother came over shortly after and thanked John for helping her girls. At the same time, she expressed her exasperation with the girls saying, "I just don't know! I swear I can't even go to the bathroom without these kids hanging onto me!" That comment concerned John a great deal. He thought to himself that he shared her "exasperation," but not with the children, rather with her and other parents who just don't understand that young children should never be left alone and especially never around a swimming pool.

****

This very popular and busy amusement and recreation park has hundreds of people in the three large pools on hot days like we had that day when lifeguard Bill pulled a young girl out after she had quietly submerged in the water. Bill was guarding the middle pool while sitting in the elevated guard stand at the deep end. It was so hot, that people were filling the pools quickly. So many people that, true "swimming" was next to impossible. It was more like standing around and splashing in the water to cool off.

Bill has seen this happen before and he noticed several small children in the shallow end and some of them were moving toward the middle and deeper water. With so many adults standing in the water, their larger bodies blocked his view and it was difficult for him to see the smaller kids behind them. Anticipating a potential problem, Bill came down from his guard stand and walked to the side of the pool so he could have a clear view of everyone.

Sure enough, that move allowed him to see a young girl who was struggling to keep her head up and she was right next to a larger adult who was not aware that she was there. As she began to sink further, Bill was able to reach in and pull her out to safety. She was not only very close to an adult who didn't notice her, she was so close to the side of the pool that Bill did not even have to go in the water. He could reach her simply by lying down on the pool deck and reaching in.

****

You would think that children would be safe in a swim class with a fully qualified swim instructor in the water with them, wouldn't you? Well, usually they are but even here, lifeguards and parents need to watch very closely.

Lifeguard John was guarding the swimming pool while Mary, the swim instructor was conducting a swim class made up of 6 pre-school age children. While there were other swimmers in the water that John had to keep an eye on, he stayed closer to the swim class swimmers than the lap swimmers because of their lack of swimming skills and potential danger.

Everyone in the swim class was wearing a floatation bubble. Additionally, they all were taught to hold onto the side of the pool when waiting their turn with the instructor. As, I'm sure you can imagine some highly active kids just can't sit still and they can't hold still on the side of the pool either.

One 2 ½ year old boy often tried to let go when he thought no one was watching. He was OK for a stroke or two as long as he was able to quickly get back and grab the wall again.

One time he let go and pushed himself away from the wall to where he could not reach it. Even with the bubble on, he sank below the surface of the water. His eyes were wide open like saucers and he was kicking and stroking as fast as he could just like he was taught. His efforts were in vein, however, because he was in a vertical position with his head completely submerged. He simply was not strong enough to keep himself afloat without the instructor's assistance.

Anticipating that this could happen, John was just one step away. He jumped in and picked the boy up, out of the water in just a few seconds and he was fine. It is not practical to believe that a swim instructor can teach and watch every student at the same time, 100% of the time. There needs to be another set of eyes watching.

****

PARENTS: Part of the fun with children is the fact that they are unpredictable but that too, can make protecting their safety challenging. Always expect the unexpected with children. "Safe" is never "Perfect." Keep watching.

LIFEGUARDS: Pay attention to your swimmers and learn their capabilities. Stay close to higher risk situations. Don't allow any blind spots to get in your way. Anticipate potential dangers so you can be a step closer to preventing a tragedy.

5 - <u>CPR WORKS!</u>

Danny was the Pool Manager and John was the Head Lifeguard at that large amusement and recreation park with the three pools. Danny was 19 and John was just 17 years old but they both took their jobs seriously and were very responsible young men. There was a corporate event going on that day with many families attending the park, so, things were pretty busy.

At some point in the afternoon, Danny noticed an 8 year old girl floating motionless in the large pool. He immediately blew his whistle, jumped in and removed the girl from the water. John responded to the whistle and as he approached, he observed Danny placing her down on the pool deck. As he laid her down, Danny called to John to get the oxygen tank. John immediately ran to the lifeguard office to retrieve the oxygen and signaled to another park employee to call 911. As John returned with the oxygen, a crowd had gathered and he had to practically fight his way through to get to the girl. Other lifeguards closed one of the pools and assisted with crowd control to give Danny and John the room they needed.

The girl had only been in the water for just a very short time, so, what caused her to stop breathing and for her heart to stop was not known for sure. Danny had begun CPR before John returned. Together, they worked as a team performing CPR. They had performed CPR on this girl for almost 20 minutes when, miraculously, she coughed and began to show renewed signs of life. She was breathing on her own! John & Danny stayed with her, assisting with the oxygen for a short while longer when the EMTs finally arrived and took over. They transported her to a nearby hospital where she ultimately recovered very well.

Both Danny and John had been trained and they practiced how to perform CPR so they would be prepared when the time came. When it came, they simply and automatically responded and did what they needed to do. Their training and practice had automatically kicked in when they needed it. It was not until all was said and done, and after they had time to realize the gravity of what they had just done, that they found themselves shaking uncontrollably until their hearts slowed back down to normal.

****

John was working full time then as the YMCA Aquatics Director but one day he came back to our pool just to say, "Hi," and visit with some old friends. He was walking along side one of the pools with Bill, who had worked for John previously and was now the Pool Manager, when they saw a scary sight.

One of the new and inexperienced lifeguards was carrying a boy about 11 years old, who appeared to be unconscious. As he held the boy in his arms, he was running toward them and calling out to Bill that the boy was not breathing.

Unfortunately, this new lifeguard had panicked (remember "lifeguards are human too") when he saw the boy in the pool and apparently forgot some of his training. He did not blow his whistle, so no one on staff knew that he had even gone into the water to rescue the boy. Additionally, rather than immediately attending to the boy where the incident occurred, he was carrying him around the pool toward the lifeguard office, wasting precious time.

Bill immediately had the guard lay the boy down and John began CPR. Unfortunately, the boy's airway was blocked and the air was not getting in. John continued the process and the boy eventually vomited and was just fine after that. Again the CPR process worked!

****

Cardio-Pulmonary Resuscitation (CPR) Works!

PARENTS: Learn CPR. Practice it and if you ever need to use it, trust that your training will allow you to respond appropriately. It may not work all the time but wouldn't you want to give your child or a friend every chance at life that you can?

LIFEGUARDS: Learn CPR. Practice it and if you ever need to use it, trust that your training will allow you to respond appropriately. It may not work all the time but everyone deserves your best effort.

6 - <u>SEIZURE DISORDERS</u>

Do you remember back in Chapter 2, "Lifeguards are Human Too," where a new lifeguard on his first day on the job, hesitated when he saw a swimmer in trouble? Head Lifeguard John ended up going in the pool to pull a boy and a girl out of the water after they had both been submerged. Well, to continue on where that chapter left off on this story, *'She was fine immediately. It took a little longer for the boy to catch his breath'*…

While John held the boy in the water at the edge of the pool so he could catch his breath, his mother ran over and quickly tried to pull him out. John stopped her and she said, "He knows how to swim if that is what you are worried about." John continued to hold him in the water, explaining to his mother that something caused him to panic and stop swimming. So John just wanted to be sure he was alright before he released him.

It was at this point that his mother explained that the boy has an anxiety condition that may have contributed to the situation. After making sure he was OK, John released the boy to his mother.

That mother's reaction reminded me of a personal experience with my own mother. As a youngster, I had a minor form of epilepsy, which I eventually outgrew. However, my well meaning mother, wanted to protect me from the embarrassment and stigma associated with epilepsy at the time, and did not report my condition to my schools. (Today, the ailment is better understood and hopefully less stigmatized). One day, my mother was soundly chastised by our school nurse when I had an epileptic seizure in junior high school.

17

Any such conditions need to be reported to the lifeguards before entering the water. As a lifeguard, I have had the parents or guardians of special needs children report to me that a child is prone to seizures which helps me be prepared. Even today, I have a swimmer who attends a water aerobics class regularly and reminds us that she has epilepsy every time she comes. We are trained on how to treat these kinds of conditions and if we know, we will be better prepared to recognize a problem and respond immediately and appropriately.

****

PARENTS: If you or your child has a physical, mental or emotional condition that could endanger them while in the water, it should be brought to the attention of the lifeguard before entering the water. And then ... watch your child.

LIFEGUARDS: Understand that it is not just a person's lack of swimming ability that causes swimming accidents. Excellent adult swimmers have become totally incapacitated by the extreme pain of a simple leg cramp. Heart attacks, strokes, epilepsy and other seizure disorders can happen to anyone, young and old. Be vigilant and alert to all swimmers as you are scanning the water.

7 - WHAT DOES A WATER-RELATED ACCIDENT LOOK LIKE?

It may not look like what you would think it should look like. Our TV's and movies all make it look like a frantic episode of splashing and thrashing around in the water with the victim going down and coming back up repeatedly. Remember the myth that it's the "*third time*" that is fatal?

To be sure, some swimmers in distress or actively drowning may splash and stroke briefly as they lift their head up to gasp for air. Unfortunately, they may not have three chances before going down for the last time. It can happen in seconds.

Many times it is silent! A child can slip underwater without a sound. There may be no yelling or splashing. Once underwater an individual can panic, breathe in the water and attempt to yell but no one will hear. Additionally, a victim can submerge once without ever resurfacing.

You have just read about several incidents here and none of them would have fit the movie version. Another misconception is that it is always fatal. All my stories here have had happy endings but it requires appropriate actions by someone who can help.

One other thing to be aware of is that many more people nearly drown than actually drown. This is sometimes called *near drowning* or *secondary drowning*.* Very serious complications can manifest themselves immediately after the incident or it may take many hours.

19

If someone has had a serious accident and is still struggling after coming out of the water and certainly anyone who required CPR should receive immediate medical attention. A hospital can monitor the full recovery over time.

Others may not exhibit symptoms for several hours after an accident. An individual successfully pulled out of the water may cough a little and seem perfectly alright but even a small amount of water that may not be cleared from the lungs can be dangerous. So, anyone who has experienced and survived a water related accident should be monitored for an extended period following the incident. If you notice any changes in personality, or energy levels or any other suspicious symptoms, seek medical attention immediately.

****

PARENTS: Knowing that an accident can happen quickly and silently, the only way to be aware of it is to *watch* your children at all times. Call 911 for a serious incident and if all appears OK after a mild incident, continue to monitor your child for any unusual behavior or changes in energy level and seek medical help immediately at the first signs of trouble.

LIFEGUARDS: Be vigilant and alert. Call 911 when warranted and suggest to the parents of a mild incident victim that they monitor the child and seek medical attention at the first signs of any unusual behavior.

8 - <u>MORE VERY IMPORTANT STUFF</u> <u>& PREVENTIVE MEASURES</u>

Through all my many years of observing swimming accidents and researching other water related tragedies, one theme continues to repeat itself over and over again. The fact is that virtually all of these accidents are preventable. And what's even better is that what we need to do to prevent them is very, very simple!

I love to swim. I learned to swim very young at a YMCA and I continue to enjoy it as often as I can. Swimming and other water activities are fun for the whole family as well as providing great exercise, sporting competition, outstanding recreation and soothing relaxation. There is no need to be afraid as long as we just learn a few simple things we all can do to be safe in the water.

None of these stories or anything mentioned here should cause anyone to avoid swimming. It is all intended to help us learn how to be safe and have those happy endings I want for us all.

I mentioned earlier that this is not a book about statistics and I don't want to dwell on them. However, I believe it is important to share some so we can learn and understand what those simple preventive measures can be. So, here is a list of 10 statistics presented by The Center for Disease Control (CDC):**

- Drowning is ***the leading cause*** of accidental injury-related death among children ages 1 – 4.
- Drowning is the second leading cause of accidental injury-related death among children 1 – 14.
- Each day in the United States 10 people drown.
- For each death caused by drowning, there are 5 nonfatal submersion accidents serious enough for the victim to be hospitalized.
- Among children ages 1 – 4 years, ***most drownings occur in residential swimming pools.***
- In nearly 9 out of 10 child-drowning deaths, ***a parent or caregiver claimed to be watching the child.***
- Seventy-seven percent of those involved in a home-drowning accident had only been missing for 5 minutes or less when found in the swimming pool. And 70% weren't expected to be in or near the pool at the time.
- 19% percent of child drowning fatalities take place in ***public pools with certified lifeguards on duty.***
- More than half of drownings among infants under age 1 occur in ***bathtubs, buckets and toilets.***
- Participation in ***formal swimming lessons can reduce the risk of drowning by 88%*** among children ages 1 – 4.

If I was to summarize what I would take away from those 10 "statistics," I would say: our youngest children are at greatest risk, so we really, really need to be watching them and watching them some more, especially around home swimming pools (ours or a neighbor's). If a child goes missing, the first place to look is in a nearby pool. We also need to be aware that tragedy can happen even at public pools with lifeguards on duty, as well as in some of the most unusual places like bathtubs, buckets and toilets which present a danger to our very little toddlers. And finally, we need to begin the swimming lessons as soon as we can.

For those who have a home pool, there are several ways to make it safe for all. First and foremost is to have a fence around the pool. Not just a fence around the yard but around the pool itself within the yard. Make sure it is appropriately locked when not supervised. You may also consider alarms for the pool itself or at the exit doors from your house so that you know immediately if a child wonders (or sneaks) out of the house.

Additionally, keep toys away from the edge of the pool. Young children are often attracted by such toys and may go too close to the pool to retrieve a toy. And consider what you will do when you have a party with other people there when you don't know their ability to swim. My daughter, who has a fence immediately around her back yard pool, had the right idea when she had a birthday party for her 5 year old son. Her son can swim but she was concerned for his friends who attended the party. She knew she could not count on the other children's parents being there and watching the pool closely. She and her husband decided to divide the party duties. He was in charge of all the yard activities outside of the pool while she, a former lifeguard, guarded the pool at all times it was open.

Inflatable toys are NOT approved personal floatation devices (PFD)! Don't use them! Those blowup tubes and rings with the cute ducky are not safe for a non-swimmer to use. Children can slide through them. A small child is not strong enough to hold on and the tubes can lose air causing them to sink along with the child. **No blowup water wings!** They too can come off and lose air.

I saw a child once with water wings on his arms when he took one off. Guess what? He went in the water and the arm with the wing floated fine but the rest of his body, including his head, was totally submerged.

23

In fact, I don't allow any blowup toys in any of my pools. Do you remember back in chapter 3 when Lifeguard John pulled a little girl, Kathy, out of the 3 foot end of the wading pool? Her mother was not paying enough attention to the pool's depths and her daughter's limitations.

Well, shortly after leaving Kathy with her mother, John observed her mother blowing up a couple of water wings and beginning to put them on Kathy. John immediately called to her to stop. He picked up an extra "puddle jumper" they had at the pool and brought that over to them for Kathy to use. He explained why the water wings were not safe. By this time her mother was quite frustrated by the whole experience and she said to John, "You must think I am the worse mother in the world. We actually have a "puddle jumper" at home but forgot to bring it with us today."

So, watch your children closely and if you are smart enough to have a safe PFD, be sure to bring it along for all swimming activities.

Speaking about "watching," the best way to watch is through "touch supervision." Touch supervision simply means that you are, at all times, close enough to the child to be able to touch him or her while watching. That means you have to _actually get in the water_ with your child. Imagine that! If your child cannot swim, letting him or her in the water without close supervision in the water with him or her is like letting your child swim alone. No one should ever swim alone.

I am often amazed when I talk to the parents of children in my swim classes who can't swim themselves. They want their children to learn how to swim but they never learned, and for some reason, are too afraid to learn now. I always encourage them to learn to swim and explain to them that their being in the water with the child supports and encourages that child's ability to learn. And we all know that the old cliché, "do as I say, not as I do," is not the most successful approach.

Here's a solution for adults afraid to learn to swim. Have a qualified instructor show you how to use a Coast Guard Approved Lifejacket. Get in the water with it and learn that you can be safe wearing a lifejacket in 3 or 4 feet of water so you can provide touch supervision to your young child. I'll bet the experience will inspire you to go the next step and take lessons so both you and your child can enjoy the fun of swimming together.

One final note about those other bodies of water we usually don't think about when we think of water safety and swimming. It only takes a few seconds for a young child to slip underwater in a bath tub. Maybe the few seconds it takes to leave to get a towel, answer the phone or the front doorbell. Please, finish the bath first, or if it is so important, take that wet baby with you.

Remember, too, empty that backyard splash pool, empty all buckets and other containers and store them out of reach. And with toddlers, keep the toilet bowl covers down.

All these things may sound like a lot but they are all very simple and easy things to do and well worth doing for a lifetime of fun in the water.

Oh, and did I say watch them closely?

That can be the most fun part.

9 - SUMMARY FOR PARENTS

First of all:

1. Learn to swim
2. Teach your children to swim
3. **Watch your children**
4. **Watch some more**

Additionally, the statistics tell us that our youngest children are at greatest risk, so we really, really need to be watching them and watching them some more, especially around home swimming pools (ours or a neighbor's). If a child goes missing, the first place to look is in a nearby pool. We also need to be aware that tragedy can happen even at public pools with lifeguards on duty, as well as in some of the most unusual places like bathtubs, buckets and toilets which present a danger to our very little toddlers. And finally, we need to begin the swimming lessons as soon as we can.

When supervising a child don't be distracted by activities like reading, playing cards, texting, mowing the lawn, talking on the phone or with others. In fact, when it comes to supervision, "touch supervision" is always best.

Drowning can happen in seconds & be silent. You can only see it if you are watching.

Know your child's limitations and the water depths so you can stop him or her before the water is over their heads.

Cardio-Pulmonary Resuscitation (CPR) Works! Learn it.

In the event of a water accident, even when all appears fine, monitor your child for any trouble signs as serious complications can manifest themselves many hours later.

Have a home pool? Think about: Fences, Locks, Alarms, and Toys (away from pool's edge)

Empty backyard splash pools, buckets and other containers, and cover the toilet bowls.

Lifeguards are **NOT** your **"Babysitters.** *You are the first line of defense for your child*.

If you or your child has a physical, mental or emotional condition that could endanger them while in the water, *notify the lifeguard before entering the water.*

NO BLOW UP / INFLATABLE TOYS!

NO ONE SHOULD EVER SWIM ALONE.

GET IN THE WATER!

IT IS MORE FUN FOR YOU & YOUR CHILD IF YOU ARE BOTH IN THE WATER.

10 - <u>SUMMARY FOR LIFEGUARDS</u>

First of all:

1. Stay alert and focused without distractions
2. Anticipate
3. React to any and all concerns – seconds count
4. Know that common sense is all too uncommon

Additionally, remember that accidents have happened in a pool just like yours.

Almost 20% of child-drowning deaths
take place in pools <u>with certified lifeguards on duty</u>.

Experienced lifeguards need to watch and help "rookies."

"Non-swimmers" are not the only ones involved in water accidents. Cramps, seizure disorders, strokes, heart attacks and simply getting tired can get swimmers in trouble. And to be sure, some swimmers in distress or actively drowning may splash around briefly but many times it is silent & only takes seconds. Be vigilant and watch everyone.

IF YOU DON'T KNOW – GO!

CARDIO-PULMONARY RESUSCITATION (CPR) WORKS – PRACTICE IT!

Call 911 when warranted and suggest to the parents of a mild incident victim to monitor the child and seek medical attention at the first signs of any unusual behavior.

Be aware of everyone in and around the pool, in an effort to anticipate potential problems so that you may be able to take action before an accident happens.

Expect the unexpected. Know that others don't think like you do. What is "Common Sense" to you, is all too often uncommon to the general public

DO NOT ALLOW BLOW-UP / INFLATABLE TOYS.

Learn the "JGL." For the vast majority of my many "saves," I found that the quickest and most effective technique is something I call the "Jump, Grab & Lift (JGL). It is not fancy or difficult & it is often overlooked in Lifeguarding Classes, but if you are working at a pool with clear water that you can stand up in with lots of small children swimming & where you can get to them quickly, it gets the job done. It is vitally important to learn the formal techniques taught in class because in other circumstances, they are much more effective. Just remember that the "JGL" is another option you have.

ENJOY YOUR LIFEGUARDING EXPERIENCE!

You are providing a very important service!

REFERENCES & ADDITIONAL INFORMATION

*WebMD:
http://www.webmd.com/parenting/news/20140602/dry-drowning-faq

**Centers for disease Control and Prevention, National Center for Injury Prevention and Control, Division of Unintentional Injury Prevention
http://www.cdc.gov/HomeandRecreationalSafety/Water-Safety/waterinjuries-factsheet.html

Edgar Snyder & Associates
www.edgarsnyder.com/swimming-pool-statistics.html

Made in the USA
Middletown, DE
25 April 2015